Introduction to Tort Law in India

By Siva Prasad Bose

Published by Joy Bose

Copyright 2022 Joy Bose

All Rights Reserved

Contents

Preface 3
Chapter 1: Introduction to Torts 5
Chapter 2: Tort of Negligence 19
Chapter 3: Tort of Nuisance 30
Chapter 4: Tort of Defamation 37
Chapter 5: Tort of Trespass 46
Chapter 6: Tort of Malicious Prosecution 62
Chapter 7: Code of Civil Procedure 66
Chapter 8: Sending a Legal Notice 69
Chapter 9: Vicarious Liability 72
Chapter 10: Consumer Protection and Torts 77
Chapter 11: Emerging Torts in the Digital Age 82
Chapter 12: Conclusion 87
About the Author 89
Other Books by Siva Prasad Bose 90

Preface

Tort law is an important component of civil law in India. It covers the cases that relate to damages caused by an individual or group to another, but which do not come under the ambit of criminal law. Examples include defamation, nuisance and trespassing. Typically, damages are awarded by the court to compensate for the loss suffered.

Tort law governs the everyday harms and wrongs that affect individuals in society — from personal injury and property damage to defamation, negligence, and civil accountability. Despite its centrality to legal redress and civil rights, tort law remains an often underappreciated area within Indian legal education and public understanding.

This book is a fresh and accessible introduction to the world of torts in India. It is designed for students, legal professionals, and general readers who seek a clear and practical overview of how tort law operates — both in theory and in the lived realities of Indian society.

Each chapter explores a key branch of tort law, enriched with Indian case law, relatable examples, and procedural insights. Whether discussing nuisance, trespass, or vicarious liability, the book shows how tort law is not merely academic but deeply connected to real-life grievances and remedies.

In a time when technological changes, urban challenges, and growing awareness of rights are reshaping legal interactions, tort law is increasingly important. From online defamation to environmental harm, from negligent services to the misuse of state power, this field continues to evolve.

This book aims to provide a strong foundation in tort principles while encouraging readers to think critically about justice, responsibility, and the evolving nature of civil wrongs in India.

Chapter 1: Introduction to Torts

In this chapter we discuss what is tort and what are the types of tort.

1.1 Necessity of Tort Law

In criminal law, when someone commits a wrong, we call it a crime. Similarly, in civil law, when a person commits a wrong, we call it a tort. Typically the wronged person files a case in a civil court to claim monetary or other damages from the wrong doer.

The term "tort" is a French equivalent of the English word "wrong" and of the Roman law term "delict". The word is derived from the Latin word "tortum" which means an act which is twisted or crooked or wrong or unlawful.

For a healthy society it is necessary to have rule of law and be free from anti-social elements and an individual should have freedom to exercise their rights without being restricted by others. Also, if there is a transgression of any right, there must be a way to compensate or to restore the right. This is essentially what is implied by the latin maxim "*ubi jus, ibi remedium*", meaning wherever there is a right, there is a remedy.

Indian legal treatment in case of torts is derived from the English law. However, there are also some differences.

Generally, there is no specific law for torts in India. The law is mostly defined on the basis of case law i.e., by citing verdicts in previous cases in Indian courts.

Examples of situations where tort law can be applied include the following:

- Consumer complaints, where the promised goods in good quality were not delivered.
- Torts by government employees acting under orders, for which the state can be held liable.
- Constitutional torts, where the state is held liable for the actions of its employees, especially when a person's constitutional rights are violated. Many of the constitutional tort petitions involving the state or government employees fall under Public Interest Litigations or PILs. PILs are intended to enable the raising of certain issues of social importance that affect a number of people in society, especially in cases where the rights of one or more underprivileged groups are being denied. The first PIL was filed in 1979. These can be filed in the high courts and supreme court under articles 32 and 226 of the Constitution of India.
- Personal injuries caused by an accident leading to permanent disability and/or loss of earnings and medical expenses, etc.

In all such cases, the damages to be awarded (once the tort is proved) are calculated based on estimation of the amount of loss to the plaintiff.

1.2 Definitions of Tort

In order to find out the factors which are necessary to constitute a tort, let us look at definitions of the term "tort" given by eminent jurists:

- Winfield: Tort is a liability that arises from the breach of a duty primarily fixed by law; the duty is towards persons generally and its breach is redressable by an action for unliquidated damages.
- Fraser: Tort is an infringement of a right in rem of a private individual giving a right of compensation at the suit of the injured party.
- Salmond: Tort is a civil wrong for which the remedy is action in common law for unliquidated damages and which is not exclusively a breach of contract or breach of Trust or other equitable obligations.
- Clark and Lindsell: A tort may be described as a wrong independent of contract for which the appropriate remedy is a common law action
- Sir Frederick Pollock: Every tort is an act or omission, not being mainly the breach of a duty arising out of a personal relation or undertaken by contract, which is related to harm, including

interference with an absolute right, whether or not measurable actual damage is suffered by a determinate person.
- Sir John Salmond further observed that every legal right implies a corresponding duty, and every breach of such duty is potentially tortious in nature.

1.3 Essential Characteristics of a Tort

The essential characteristics of a tort are as follows:

- **Wrongful act or omission**: An action by a person will be wrongful when it violates some legal right of another person. Tort liability arises when a wrongful act is a cause of violation of a legal right or a breach of duty.
- **Legal damage**: Legal damage is an important element of tort. However, a legal damage cannot be said to be identical with actual damage, meaning that actual damage may or may not have occurred to the plaintiff. It is not pecuniary in nature.
- **Legal remedy**: another element of a tort is that it must provide for legal remedy. The breach of tort must be redressable by an action for unliquidated damages. Apart from unliquidated damages, injunction (where the court orders a person to cease an action) and restitution (restoring the past state of affairs, such as rejoining employment in case

someone is fired from a job) are some of the other possible remedies.

1.4 Types of Tort

Tort liability exists for three major categories of conduct: intentional wrongs, negligence, and activities for which strict liability is imposed.

Intentional wrong: This occurs when a person acts with intent to injure a person, their property or both. For example, if A is angry at B, so they intentionally smash the windshield of B's car.

Intentional torts may also be crimes. Usually in these cases, the defendant can be pursued by the state as well as sued by the plaintiff. However, punishing a criminal does not usually make up for further harm to the victim.

A civil tort action is used to recover monetary damages.

Negligence: The most common type of tort is negligence. Negligence is an unintentional tort. It occurs when a person's failure to use reasonable care causes harm. For example, if a drunk driver accidentally hits a pedestrian, the driver is negligent, even though the driver did not intend to actually hurt the pedestrian.

Strict Liability: Strict liability is different from both negligence and intentional wrong. It applies when the defendant is engaged in an activity so dangerous that there is a serious risk or harm, even if they act with utmost care. In a strict liability, there is no need to prove that the defendant was either negligent or intended to cause harm in order to recover damages. For example, demolishing buildings is so dangerous that contractors are automatically responsible if a passerby is injured.

Three groups of people face strict liability:

- Owners of dangerous animals
- People who engage in highly dangerous activities
- Manufacturers and sellers of defective consumer products

However, it is important to note that not all injuries to a person or their property can lead to a recovery under tort law. In some instances, harmful behavior may not be a tort. In others, the person causing the harm may have legal "defense" to a tort action. Also, the defendant may be liable, but may simply be too poor to pay for the harm, and therefore no recovery is possible.

1.5 Civil and Criminal Law in India

Tort law is a form of civil law. Civil law deals with disputes between individuals. In a civil court case, the party that was harmed may sue the party that caused the harm. This differs from criminal law, in which the state brings charges against the accused. Criminal law deals with actions that are defined as crimes against the public, even if there is an individual victim.

However, the same actions by a party may be liable for both a civil and criminal court case. The way these are treated under Indian law is however slightly different.

The civil courts in India use "balance of probabilities" as the standard of proof. This standard requires that more than 50% of the weight of the evidence be in favor of the winning party. The civil standard is easier to meet than the criminal standard, which requires that the guilt be proven beyond "reasonable doubt".

This is appropriate because the penalties for those found liable in a civil action are less severe than the penalties for those found guilty in a crime. A person does not go to jail for committing a tort, but instead pays damages to the injured or harmed party.

1.6 Taking One's Case to Court

In some situations, the same action can be both a tort as well as a crime. This may lead to two separate actions against the defendant. For example, M may be sued for driving while intoxicated and killing a policeman. M may also be charged with the crime of negligent homicide and manslaughter for his actions. The criminal case will be brought by the state, which must prove that M was guilty beyond a reasonable doubt. This is called the "standard of proof". The victim's family may also sue M in a civil court. In the civil case, the victim's family will attempt to recover damages for the wrongful death.

The OJ Simpson murder case in 1994 in the United States is a perfect example that showed the difference between a civil and criminal case. In this case, Simpson was found not guilty of murdering his wife and her friend in the criminal case, but found guilty in the civil case and had to pay damages to the family of the killed.

1.7 Important Maxims in the Law of Torts

Two important maxims in the law of torts are as follows:

- *Injuria sine damnum (injury without damage):* It means that if there has been a violation of a legal right, the same is actionable and damages payable, irrespective of whether there is actual harm to the plaintiff. The affected party can bring a civil proceeding in a court of law raising a tort liability, because every violation of a legal right has to be redressed. This is also exemplified in the principle *ubi jus, ibi remedium* or where there is a right there is a remedy.
- *Damnum sine injuria (damage without injury):* This covers the acts which though harmful are not wrongful and give no right of action to them who suffers from their effects. In such a case, where the

person's legal rights are not violated even though they may have suffered losses due to some actions of another person, no remedy is applicable and no damages are payable to such a person. For example, if a person opens a shop selling toys next to another shop selling similar toys, it is a loss to the original shop since some of their customers may be lost to the new toys shop, but their legal rights are not violated.

1.8 Characteristics of the Law of Torts

The main characteristics of the law of torts are as follows:

- A tort is a private wrong, which infringes the legal right of an individual or specific group of individuals.
- The person who commits a tort is called a "tortfeasor" or wrongdoer.
- The place of trial is a civil court
- Tort litigation is compoundable i.e., the plaint can withdraw and settle the suit filed by them.
- Tort is a species of civil injury or wrong.
- Tort is other than a breach of contract. For breaches of contract, contract law is applicable and not tort law.

- The remedy in tort is unliquidated damage (where the amount of damage is determined by the court) or other equitable relief granted to the injured party.

1.9 Wrongful Acts Recognized in the Law of Torts

The following wrongful acts are recognized in the law of torts:

- Negligence
- Nuisance
- Defamation
- Trespass (including trespass to the person as well as to property)
- Malicious prosecution

1.10 Types of legal remedies for torts

The law provides for different kinds of legal remedies if a tort is proved to have happened. Such remedies are given to the persons who have suffered a damage or loss because of the tort, and include the following:

- **Damages**: The court may grant the affected party an amount of money because of the damage caused by the tort. This amount could be corresponding to their loss because of the tort or can be a nominal amount even if no actual damages are proved.

- **Injunction**: The court may grant a temporary or permanent injunction to stop the guilty party from doing or continuing some action that constituted the tort, and thus grant relief to the affected party.
- **Restitution of property**: In case the affected party has lost some property because of the tort, the court can grant the restitution of the lost property. This can include both moveable and immoveable property.

In addition, if the tort contains some criminal elements that are covered under the Indian Penal Code or IPC, then the corresponding criminal charges and punishments shall also be applied. As mentioned, the same action can lead to both a civil and criminal liability, and can lead to two separate court cases for each.

1.11 Importance of Tort Law in Everyday Life

Tort law affects us more than we realize in our daily lives. From slipping on a wet floor at a shop, to suffering due to a neighbour's construction noise, to reputational harm from a false social media post—torts are all around us. Understanding tort law empowers individuals to seek compensation and discourages negligent or harmful behaviour in society.

Many common disputes that seem personal or social in nature—such as a tenant damaging a landlord's property or a local factory polluting a stream—actually fall within the domain of torts. Therefore, basic awareness of tort law can help individuals protect their rights and resolve issues more effectively.

1.12 Torts and Fundamental Rights

Though torts are private wrongs, Indian courts have increasingly drawn connections between tortious harm and violations of fundamental rights:

- Custodial violence → Right to life (Article 21)
- Environmental pollution → Right to health and clean environment
- State negligence in accidents → Constitutional torts jurisprudence

This intersection strengthens the remedial powers of courts and broadens access to justice.

1.13 Why Tort Law is Underdeveloped in India

Despite its relevance, tort law remains relatively underdeveloped in India compared to criminal or contract law. This is due to several factors:

- **Lack of codification**: Tort law in India is largely based on common law and court judgments, making it less accessible.

- **Delay and cost of civil litigation**: Victims often find the civil court process slow, expensive, and intimidating.

- **Awareness gap**: Many citizens are unaware of their rights or confuse torts with crimes.

- **Alternative remedies preferred**: People often prefer filing police complaints or pursuing consumer forums for quicker relief.

Legal education, simplified procedures, and judicial reforms could greatly expand the role of tort law in India.

1.14 Emerging Role of Tort Law in Modern India

With the rise of public interest litigation (PIL), judicial activism, and expanding notions of rights under Article 21 of the Constitution, tort principles are being invoked more frequently. Notable developments include:

- **Constitutional torts**: Compensation for state abuse or custodial violence.

- **Environmental torts**: Courts have awarded damages for pollution, deforestation, and industrial disasters.

- **Medical negligence**: Increasing awareness and litigation in healthcare malpractice.

- **Mass torts and class actions**: In large-scale disasters (e.g., Bhopal Gas Tragedy), tort principles are applied collectively.

Thus, while tort law is still evolving in India, it has significant potential to uphold justice and accountability in a wide range of civil wrongs.

1.15 Conclusion

Tort law begins as a private remedy, but its foundations — particularly in protecting life, dignity, and personal property — extend naturally into concepts of negligence. In the next chapter, we explore how negligence, the most widely invoked tort, forms the backbone of modern tort litigation in India.

In the following chapters, we shall discuss each of the types of torts, such as negligence and nuisance, in more detail.

Chapter 2: Tort of Negligence

In this chapter we discuss the tort of negligence. This is one of the most common type of tort.

2.1 What is Negligence

Negligence simply means being careless toward others and thereby causing injury to others.

A person can be held liable for negligence if he is under a duty of care, such duty of care is breached and the breach results in some damage. For example, a drunk car driver crashing into another car unintentionally and by mistake can be a case of negligence. A damage to another's property caused by a young kid who is unable to distinguish right from wrong may, depending on the circumstance, be classed as negligence.

In common English, the word negligence has connotations of being forgetful or lack of proper diligence. In tort law, we evaluate negligence related to the conduct of a person. In civil cases, the law is more concerned with damage to the affected party than the intent of the person who caused the damage. Negligence is conduct that falls below the standard established by law for protecting others against unreasonable risks of harm. Even a person who is otherwise careful may perform a negligent action or one that causes a harm.

Everyone has a general duty to exercise reasonable care towards other persons and their property. Law of negligence deals with the case where a person's conduct violates the requirement of exercising reasonable care. For example, if an electrician does not exercise care when fixing a faulty power connection and one gets an electric shock or other accident as a result, one can sue them for damages for breaching the standard of reasonable care. Negligent conduct can hold both in performing an action or not performing an action such as that causes harm.

Negligence is the absence of proper care, caution and diligence as under the circumstances which reasonable and ordinary prudence would require to be exercised.

There is a difference between negligence and contributory negligence. Negligence is contributory when and only when it directly and proximately induces the injury in whole or in part. Contributory negligence is the negligence not avoiding the circumstances arising from the negligence of some other person, when means and opportunity are afforded to do so.

2.2 Conditions for Negligence

Generally speaking, negligence is a very broad term. To hold a person liable for negligence as per law of torts, the following three conditions must be proved in a court of law:

- **Duty of care**: The defendant owed a duty of care. This includes a legal duty to exercise ordinary care and skill.
- **Duty towards the petitioner**: The duty of care should be towards the plaintiff or affected person, who is suing the person who had the duty of care in the court of law.
- **Breach of duty**: The defendant's conduct made a breach of that duty or violated the standard of care expected of them.
- **Causation**: The breach of duty to care towards the plaintiff or petitioner was the direct cause of the harm and damage caused to the plaintiff.
- **Damages**: The plaintiff suffered actual damages as a result of the breach of duty to care. These can include material damages such as damages to property, damage to one's well-being or damage to one's reputation.

These conditions must be proven if a civil lawsuit for negligence is brought by the affected party upon the defendant.

However, there are also some defenses against these conditions that the person accused of negligence can prove. Such defenses include the following:

- An inevitable accident that could not be avoided that caused the damage
- An act of God such as an earthquake or floods

- Proving that the petitioner or plaintiff himself also had some contributory negligence in causing the damages.
- Proving that the accused person acted in self-defense in some way, to defend his own health and well-being or his property.

2.3 Negligence under Indian laws

The tort of negligence in Indian law has been derived from the laws of England. Under Indian law, a skilled professional may be found guilty of negligence if they have not performed their tasks at the level of skill expected of them. This could be in either of the following cases:

- They did not possess the required skills for the tasks
- They possessed the skills but did not exercise the skills for the task at hand

The tort of negligence can be used by consumers to sue companies providing defective products or services, in consumer courts as well as normal courts in India.

In law, negligence means the careless conduct in commission or omission of an act connoting duty, breach and damage suffered by the person to whom the plaintiff owes a duty of care [1997 (9) SCC 552]. The expression 'negligence' means breach of a legal duty to care [AIR 2002 SC 2864].

Negligence means either subjectively a careless state of mind or objectively a careless conduct. It is not an absolute term but is a relative one. It is rather a comparative term to determining whether negligence exists in a particular case, and all the surrounding facts and circumstances have to be taken into account [2003 (8) SCC 731].

One of the ingredients of negligence is there must be a duty to take care. The standard of care that the law enjoins is governed by the knowledge and skill that the office or occupation requires by the magnitude of the task and the gravity of the consequences that are likely to ensure if the required degree of care is not exercised. [AIR 1965 Allahabad 233, 236].

2.6 Medical Negligence

Medical negligence is one of the most important and sensitive areas of tort law in India. It arises when a healthcare provider breaches their duty of care, causing injury or death to a patient. Courts have emphasized that while doctors are not expected to guarantee cures, they are expected to maintain a reasonable standard of care.

Key Case Laws:

- **Jacob Mathew v. State of Punjab (2005)**: The Supreme Court held that negligence must be proved and cannot be presumed. Doctors are not criminally liable unless gross negligence is established.

- **Kusum Sharma v. Batra Hospital (2010)**: Reiterated that a balance must be struck between protecting doctors and upholding patients' rights.

Patients who suffer due to wrong diagnosis, surgical errors, or lack of consent may seek compensation under tort law or through consumer forums.

2.7 Contributory and Comparative Negligence

Negligence may not always be one-sided. In some cases, the injured party may have contributed to their own harm. This is known as **contributory negligence**.

- Under traditional common law, any contributory negligence could completely bar recovery.
- Modern Indian courts lean towards **comparative negligence**, where damages are apportioned based on the degree of fault.

Example:

If a pedestrian crosses the road carelessly and is hit by a speeding car, both may be held partially liable.

2.8 Gross Negligence and Recklessness

Gross negligence is a more severe form of negligence and implies a willful disregard for safety. It often borders on recklessness and may attract punitive damages.

Examples:

- A school failing to repair broken playground equipment despite repeated complaints.
- A driver running red lights repeatedly and causing injury.

While ordinary negligence leads to compensatory damages, gross negligence may justify higher penalties to deter future conduct.

2.9 Industrial and Occupational Negligence

Employers have a duty to provide a safe working environment. Industrial negligence occurs when workers are exposed to unsafe conditions, defective machinery, or harmful substances.

Relevant legal provisions may overlap with:

- **Factories Act, 1948**
- **Employees' Compensation Act, 1923**

Notable Example:

- **M.C. Mehta v. Union of India (Oleum Gas Leak Case, 1987)**: Expanded the principle of strict liability in hazardous industries and introduced the idea of absolute liability in India.

2.10 Prevention and Risk Management

Negligence can often be avoided through simple preventive measures:

- Adequate training of staff
- Installation of warning signs
- Periodic safety audits
- Regular inspection and maintenance

Individuals and institutions alike must adopt a culture of responsibility and risk awareness to minimize the occurrence of negligence-based harm.

2.11 Negligence in Educational Institutions

Educational institutions, including schools and colleges, owe a duty of care to students under their supervision. Breaches in safety standards, bullying, lack of adequate staff, or neglect in emergency situations may amount to negligence.

Examples:

- Inadequate safety during sports activities
- Failure to address medical emergencies
- Lack of supervision during excursions

Parents can initiate tort claims for injuries or psychological trauma caused due to the institution's negligence.

2.12 Public Authority Negligence

Negligence by government agencies or public authorities—such as municipal bodies, public hospitals, or law enforcement—can give rise to liability when their actions or omissions cause harm to citizens.

Examples:
- Poorly maintained roads causing accidents
- Delayed ambulance response by public health authorities
- Failure to prevent known hazards like open drains or unsafe construction

Courts in India have recognized such negligence and in many cases awarded compensation under tort law and constitutional remedies.

2.13 Strict Liability in the Context of Modern Industries

Today, strict liability principles are invoked in sectors such as:

- Chemical industries dealing with hazardous waste
- Nuclear power plants and radiation leakage risks
- Oil and gas pipelines, especially during explosions or leakage
- Artificial intelligence or autonomous systems (emerging domain)

The 1987 Oleum Gas Leak judgment evolved strict liability into absolute liability in India, removing exceptions in the case of inherently dangerous activities.

Modern cases continue to cite this principle when industrial or digital activities threaten public safety.

2.14 Doctrine of Res Ipsa Loquitur in Medical and Public Service Context

The principle of "Res Ipsa Loquitur"—"the thing speaks for itself"—is increasingly applied in medical negligence and public infrastructure failure cases.

Examples:

- Surgical instruments left in a patient's body
- Collapse of a newly constructed bridge or road

In such cases, negligence is presumed unless the defendant can explain otherwise. This shifts the burden of proof and supports claimants in complex technical scenarios.

2.15 Conclusion

The tort of negligence is foundational to civil wrongs and continues to evolve in response to societal needs. From workplaces and hospitals to schools and public services, negligence claims act as tools for accountability. Greater awareness, better institutional practices, and judicial activism are strengthening this area of law in India.

Negligence may be invisible but leaves real harm in its wake. When harm arises not from careless behaviour, but from consistent interference with property or comfort, we enter the realm of nuisance — the subject of our next chapter.

Chapter 3: Tort of Nuisance

In this chapter we discuss the tort of nuisance.

3.1 What is Nuisance

Nuisance as a tort means the unlawful interference with a person's use of enjoyment of land, or some right over or in connection with it. The interference may be by any way such as noise, vibrations, heat, smoke, fumes, water, gas, electricity, excavations or disease producing germs. This can also include hurting one's feelings or sentiments by displaying or broadcasting some objectionable material.

For example, making loud noise in a normally quiet neighborhood at odd hours of the night may constitute a nuisance, since it interferes with the neighbor's right to enjoy peace in their own property. Same goes for releasing smoke or gas, which affects the neighbors' right to the comfort of clean air.

The tort of nuisance includes some injury or obstruction to the person's enjoyment of their property, however it does not include trespass or occupation by another person of the property itself.

The Indian penal code defines nuisance as any act that causes an injury, danger or annoyance to the people who are staying in the property or living close to the property.

It also includes injury, obstruction, danger or annoyance to anybody who is using a public right, such as a public road or facility open to the public. This mainly refers to criminal nuisance. However, if some types of nuisance do not meet the standard of criminal nuisance, they may be included in the tort of civil nuisance.

3.2 Types of Nuisances

Nuisance may be of two types: a public nuisance or a private nuisance.

- Public nuisance is interfering with the rights of the public at large.
- Private nuisance is caused when someone interferes with the use or enjoyment of some rights of a person and inflicts damage only to that person.

Public nuisance is a crime while private nuisance is a civil wrong, covered under tort law. The punishment for a public nuisance can be a term of imprisonment or a fine, while the remedy for a private nuisance can include damages being awarded or an injunction by the court.

3.3 Conditions to prove nuisance

The conditions to prove that the tort of nuisance has occurred include the following:

- Wrongful actions by the person accused of causing nuisance
- Proof that some kind of damage has occurred as a result of the wrongful acts. This can include loss or inconvenience or annoyance in the enjoyment of their property.

3.4 Indian laws related to criminal nuisance

There are a few sections in the Indian Penal Code (IPC) related to criminal nuisance.

Section 268 of IPC on Public Nuisance states:

A person is guilty of a public nuisance who does any act or is guilty of an illegal omission which causes any common injury, danger or annoyance to the public or to the people in general who dwell or occupy property in the vicinity, or which must necessarily cause injury, obstruction, danger or annoyance to persons who may have occasion to use any public right. A common nuisance is not excused on the ground that it causes some convenience or advantage.

IPC Section 290 defines the punishment for causing public nuisance. It states as follows:

IPC 290 - Whoever commits a public nuisance in any case not otherwise punishable by this Code, shall be punished with fine which may extend to two hundred rupees.

For example, if a neighbor does a party that makes a loud noise and disturbs the neighborhood at late hours of the night, this might come under criminal nuisance and the police might be called.

3.5 Public Interest and Environmental Nuisance

Nuisance can also extend to broader issues affecting the community at large, especially when it comes to environmental pollution, noise, or public health. These issues, though not directed at a specific individual, affect public welfare and are actionable.

Examples:

- Illegal dumping of industrial waste in a residential area
- Loudspeakers used beyond permissible limits
- Air pollution caused by factories in urban zones

Courts in India have acknowledged environmental nuisance as a serious concern. In **Subhash Kumar v. State of Bihar (1991)**, the Supreme Court recognized the right to clean water and air as part of Article 21 of the Constitution.

3.6 Nuisance in Urban Residential Societies

With the growth of urban housing societies, new forms of nuisance have emerged:

- Excessive noise from neighbors
- Improper garbage disposal
- Obstruction of light or ventilation
- Unauthorized commercial activities in residential zones

Residents' associations may seek injunctions or compensation through civil suits or consumer forums. Awareness of municipal bylaws and housing regulations can also help manage such disputes.

3.7 Defences in Nuisance Cases

Defendants in nuisance claims may raise certain defences:

- **Prescriptive right**: If the nuisance-causing activity has been ongoing for over 20 years without complaint.
- **Statutory authority**: Actions carried out under lawful government authority may be exempt.
- **Consent**: If the plaintiff had knowingly accepted the nuisance.

However, these defences are not absolute and may be overruled if public interest or fundamental rights are affected.

3.8 Remedies in Nuisance Cases

Indian courts offer multiple remedies in nuisance cases:

- **Injunction**: To restrain the continuation of the nuisance.
- **Damages**: Compensation for injury, loss of enjoyment, or inconvenience.
- **Abatement**: Self-help remedy allowing the plaintiff to remove the nuisance (subject to legal limits).

3.9 Conclusion

The tort of nuisance continues to evolve as societal expectations of comfort, health, and environment rise. While traditionally focused on land-related disputes, nuisance law today addresses urban, environmental, and even digital disturbances. A well-informed citizenry and proactive judiciary are key to ensuring a balance between rights and responsibilities in a crowded and complex society.

Nuisance affects comfort; defamation affects reputation. If tort law protects dignity as well as property, then understanding defamation becomes essential — as we now explore in the next chapter.

Chapter 4: Tort of Defamation

In this chapter we discuss the tort of defamation.

4.1 What is Defamation

A defamatory statement or defamation is one which harms the reputation of a person by exposing them to hatred, contempt or ridicule, which tends to reduce the respect of members of the society towards that person or induce hostility towards them. It can be in written or spoken form. It is usually intentional, i.e., done with the intent to malign the person's reputation.

Article 19(1) of the Indian constitution protects the freedom of speech and the right of citizens of India to express their views freely. However, this right is subject to restrictions such as in case of defamatory statements. The article 19(2) states as follows:

(2) Nothing in sub clause (a) of clause (1) shall affect the operation of any existing law, or prevent the State from making any law, in so far as such law imposes reasonable restrictions on the exercise of the right conferred by the said sub clause in the interests of the sovereignty and integrity of India, the security of the State, friendly relations with foreign States, public order, decency or morality or in relation to contempt of court, defamation or incitement to an offence

The law on defamation in India seeks to drive a balance between the constitutional protected right to free speech and the need to protect a person's reputation from harm.

4.2 Types of Defamation

There are two types of defamation which are as follows:
- **Libel**: it is the publication of a defamatory statement in some permanent form, such as writing or printing an article in a newspaper or sharing in social media.
- **Slander**: it is the publication of a defamatory statement in a transient and temporary form, such as by spoken words.

In English law, both of these types of defamation are treated differently. However, the laws for both types of defamation are the same in India: both libel and slander are criminal offenses.

4.3 Conditions of Defamation

The following are the conditions to prove to the court that defamation has occurred in India:
- There must be a defamatory statement that is made

- The said statement must be about a person or a specific group of persons, not to a broad class of people
- The statement must be published in oral or written form and accessible by a third person

In addition, the following conditions are generally needed before a defamation suit can be successful:

- The statement should be defamatory in nature e.g. which can harm the reputation
- The statement must be untrue
- The statement should be made with a malicious intention
- The statement must cause harm to the reputation of the plaintiff or some other harm, such as cause them to lose their job or lose customer sales in their business.
- The statement should not be made by a member of parliament or another privileged person. In India, MPs during discussion in parliament and some other privileged persons are protected from defamation lawsuits.

The defendant, i.e., the person who is alleged to make the defamatory statement, can defend themselves by proving that the statement was true, or that it was made in public interest in good faith based on a true incident.

4.4 Burden of proof in a suit of defamation

In case a defamation suit is brought in the court, the burden of proof lies on the plaintiff, i.e., the person who has filed the lawsuit in the court. They must prove that the statement made was untrue and caused harm to them in some way.

4.5 IPC Sections for Criminal Defamation in India

As with most other types of tort, defamation comes under both civil law and criminal law in India. As in all cases, for a criminal offence, the burden of proof is higher and has to be beyond all reasonable doubt, while for the civil case it is only to be proved on the balance of probabilities that defamation has occurred.

Under criminal law, defamation comes under sections 499 and 500 of the Indian Penal Code or IPC. The defamed person can file a criminal case for defamation in court. Intentional act of defamation is punishable by imprisonment as defined in Section 500 of the IPC.

Defamation is a bailable, non-cognizable and compoundable offence under the IPC.

The IPC sections are as follows:

499. Defamation.—Whoever, by words either spoken or intended to be read, or by signs or by visible representations, makes or publishes any imputation concerning any person intending to harm, or knowing or having reason to believe that such imputation will harm, the reputation of such person, is said, except in the cases hereinafter expected, to defame that person.

Explanation 1.—It may amount to defamation to impute anything to a deceased person, if the imputation would harm the reputation of that person if living, and is intended to be hurtful to the feelings of his family or other near relatives.

Explanation 2.—It may amount to defamation to make an imputation concerning a company or an association or collection of persons as such.

Explanation 3.—An imputation in the form of an alternative or expressed ironically, may amount to defamation.

Explanation 4.—No imputation is said to harm a person's reputation, unless that imputation directly or indirectly, in the estimation of others, lowers the moral or intellectual character of that person, or lowers the character of that person in respect of his caste or of his calling, or lowers the credit of that person, or causes it to be believed that the body of that person is in a loathsome state, or in a state generally considered as disgraceful.

The IPC section 500 defines the punishment for criminal defamation.

500. Punishment for defamation.—Whoever defames another shall be punished with simple imprisonment for a *term which may extend to two years, or with fine, or with both.*

4.6 Procedure for Civil Defamation

For a civil defamation lawsuit, the normal civil court procedure takes place. It involves filing the case in the court, sending notice to the defendant, presentation of witnesses, arguments by both parties and the final judgment or verdict of the court, which can include remedies such as an amount of money as damages being awarded to the party who was defamed.

4.7 Defamation and Freedom of Speech

Defamation laws must be balanced carefully with the right to freedom of speech guaranteed under Article 19(1)(a) of the Constitution. Indian courts have recognized that while free expression is a cornerstone of democracy, it is not absolute and must respect the reputation of others.

In **Subramanian Swamy v. Union of India (2016)**, the Supreme Court upheld the constitutionality of criminal defamation under Sections 499 and 500 of the IPC, observing that reputation is an integral part of an individual's dignity.

Thus, a statement may be protected as fair comment or satire but still become actionable if it crosses into malicious falsehood.

4.8 Online Defamation and Social Media

The rise of digital platforms has led to a surge in cases of online defamation. Tweets, YouTube videos, blogs, and WhatsApp forwards can all give rise to civil or criminal defamation claims.

Challenges include:

- Rapid viral spread of defamatory content
- Anonymous or foreign-based authors
- Jurisdictional complexities
- Difficulty in obtaining takedown orders quickly

Remedies for online defamation include civil suits for damages, criminal complaints, and petitions for takedown under the IT Act and intermediary rules.

4.9 Corporate and Institutional Defamation

Organizations and companies also have reputational interests and can sue for defamation when false statements harm their business or credibility.

Examples:

- False reports about a company's financial fraud
- Malicious reviews or news articles without factual basis

However, courts expect a higher threshold of proof and often distinguish between fair criticism and defamation.

In **Tata Sons Ltd. v. Greenpeace (2011)**, the Delhi High Court ruled that exaggerated criticism, while distasteful, may fall under artistic expression rather than actionable defamation.

4.10 Defamation Defences in Depth

The following defences are particularly relevant:

- **Truth**: Complete defence if the statement is true and in public interest.
- **Fair Comment**: Must be an opinion (not a fact) on a matter of public interest.
- **Privilege**: Absolute privilege applies in Parliament and courts; qualified privilege applies in responsible journalism or official duties.
- **Consent**: If the plaintiff consented to publication, the claim fails.

4.11 Practical Tips for Avoiding Defamation Claims

- Verify facts before publishing or sharing controversial content
- Label opinions clearly as such
- Use disclaimers where needed
- Exercise caution when naming individuals or institutions
- Remove defamatory content promptly if notified

4.12 Conclusion

In a world of instant communication and digital reach, defamation law serves as a necessary check on misuse of speech. As India navigates between upholding individual reputation and fostering robust public discourse, tort law continues to provide a nuanced framework for resolving such tensions.

While defamation protects reputation, trespass protects the sanctity of physical and private space. In the next chapter, we consider how even the slightest intrusion may become a legal wrong.

Chapter 5: Tort of Trespass

In this chapter we discuss the tort of trespass.

5.1 What is Trespass

Trespass is an unlawful intrusion that interferes with a person or property. Specifically, it is a negligent or intentional act made by an individual that can cause injury to another person or their property without lawful justification, no matter how slight. It includes assault or threats made to a person, as well as trespass upon someone's property.

The use of the term injury here means a violation of one's right and not actual physical harm or loss.

5.2 Forms of Trespass

Trespass in law is of two main forms or types:

1. **Trespass to a person**: This includes even causing a slight harm to any person's body through assault or battery. This also includes threatening a person with harm.

2. **Trespass to property**: This includes trespass to chattels or moveable property as well as trespass to immoveable property. It typically applies to tangible property and allows the owners of such property to seek relief when a

third party intentionally, carelessly or recklessly interferes or meddles with the owner's possession of such moveable or immoveable property.

5.3 Definition of Trespass

Trespass includes an unexcused intrusion or interference on a person's body or the improper use or possession of property belonging to another person. This can be a basis of intentional tort.

An unlawful act committed against the person or property of another person, especially wrongful entry on a person's real property that directly interferes with their possession of the property, can be termed as trespass.

In common English, trespass refers to an unlawful or unwarranted intrusion into the land of another, including unlawful entry into the land or staying on it or making an illegal construction on the land, and a transgression of laws or rights.

The term trespass has been used by lawyers and laymen in three different senses of the term:

- In its widest sense it includes any wrongful act: any infringement or transgression of the rule of right
- In a narrower sense it means any legal wrong for which an appropriate remedy exists

- In its narrowest sense it means a particular kind of trespass viz. the tort of trespass to land

5.4 Civil and Criminal Trespass

While tortious trespass is a civil wrong, criminal trespass under Section 441 of the Indian Penal Code (IPC) involves intent to commit an offence or intimidate, insult, or annoy. Trespass can be both civil and criminal.

- **Criminal trespass** is where the occupier threatens the owner of the property or commits assault on a person. This is covered under the sections of the IPC or Indian Penal Code.
- **Civil trespass**: Where criminal trespass does not apply, it is civil trespass and comes under tort law.

All trespass may not be classed as criminal trespass, unless violence and intimidation are involved. If it is not criminal then civil remedies, such as an injunction or damages awarded as a result of a civil court case, may be applied.

Key differences include:

Feature	Civil Trespass	Criminal Trespass
Forum	Civil court	Criminal court
Intent	Not necessary	Must involve wrongful intent

| Outcome | Compensation, injunction | Imprisonment, fine |

Victims may pursue both remedies if the facts support both civil and criminal liability.

The two main forms of trespass are trespass to person and trespass to property.

- **Trespass to the person** includes assault and other harm to the person's body. It also includes threats made by one person to another.
- **Trespass to property** is an act by someone where they don't have rights on one's property, yet they illegally enter it, occupy it, or build some illegal construction upon it, without consent of the owner, or prevent the actual owner, from using it. This can be, for example, by installing gates, locks or other construction. In trespass, someone illegally gains entry to and occupies the property that legally belongs to someone else, against their will.

There is also a trespass called house trespass where a person, such as a neighbor commits criminal trespass on a portion or whole of one's house where one is currently staying.

5.5 Types of Trespass in Modern Context

While traditional trespass focuses on physical entry into land, courts are increasingly dealing with broader interpretations:

- **Trespass to High-Rise Flats or Gated Communities**: Unauthorized entry by salespersons, political agents, or protestors may be treated as trespass depending on community rules.
- **Drone Trespass**: Use of drones to hover over private property may constitute aerial trespass and invasion of privacy.
- **Trespass by Pollution**: In some rulings, persistent environmental damage like chemical seepage or noise has been viewed as a form of indirect trespass.

These modern contexts illustrate how tort law adapts to changing lifestyles and technology.

5.6 Remedies available for the tort of trespass

If the court finds that the tort of trespass has indeed occurred, it can provide a few types of remedies:

- **Damages**: The court can provide a sum of money to be given from the trespassing party to the affected party as damages
- **Injunctions**: The court can pronounce an injunction to stop the trespasser from occupying the land or doing any such other actions.

- **Restitution or Eviction**: In cases where illegal occupation continues.

In India, courts may grant even nominal damages if no substantial harm is shown, simply to affirm the right to exclusive possession.

5.7 Indian laws on criminal trespass

Sections 350 and 351 of the Indian Penal code deals with trespass to person, specifically in case of assault.

Section 441 of Indian Penal Code IPC deals with criminal trespass to property, and 447 for punishment for criminal trespass. Section 442 deals with house trespass.

Section 133 of IPC describes the procedure for removal of nuisances of illegal construction by neighbors.

The sections 441, 442 and 447 of IPC are discussed in the following subsections.

5.8 IPC 350 and 351 on Trespass by Assault

IPC section 350 states the following:

350. Criminal force.—Whoever intentionally uses force to any person, without that person's consent, in order to the committing of any offence, or intending by the use of such force to cause, or knowing it to be likely that by the use of such force he will cause injury, fear or annoyance to the person to whom the force is used, is said to use criminal force to that other.

The IPC 351 states the following:

351. Assault.—Whoever makes any gesture, or any preparation intending or knowing it to be likely that such gesture or preparation will cause any person present to apprehend that he who makes that gesture or preparation is about to use criminal force to that person, is said to commit an assault.

Explanation.—Mere words do not amount to an assault. But the words which a person uses may give to his gestures or preparation such a meaning as may make those gestures or preparations amount to an assault.

5.9 IPC 441 Criminal trespass

The IPC 441 states the following:

Whoever enters into or upon property in the possession of another with intent to commit an offence or to intimidate, insult or annoy any person in possession of such property, or having lawfully entered into or upon such property, unlawfully remains there with intent thereby to intimidate, insult or annoy any such person, or with intent to commit an offence, is said to commit "criminal trespass".

5.10 IPC 442. House trespass

IPC 442 states the following:

Whoever commits criminal trespass by enter-ing into or remaining in any building, tent or vessel used as a human dwelling or any building used as a place for worship, or as a place for the custody of property, is said to commit "house-trespass".

5.11 IPC 447. Punishment for criminal trespass

The IPC 447 states the following:

Whoever commits criminal trespass shall be punished with imprisonment of either description for a term which may extend to three months, with fine or which may extend to five hundred rupees, or with both.

5.12 Steps to take if someone trespasses one's property

If someone illegally occupies a part or whole of one's property, the following steps can be taken:

a. Obtain photos, videos and other proof of the trespassed property. If the person has made any illegal constructions on the property, get proof of that as well.

b. In case of criminal trespass or trespass with threats and intimidation, visit the nearest police station and/or file a written complaint, asking for help and protection. Include documentation and proofs such as photos.

c. Send a legal notice to the person who has trespassed, asking them to vacate the illegally trespassed property, failing which legal proceedings will be initiated.

d. File a lawsuit or writ petition before the courts (such as district court or high court) requesting direction to the police and other authorities for eviction of the occupier (neighbor who has trespassed) from the property and restoration of possession of that property to us.

e. File a suit before the courts requesting to pass an immediate stay / injunction against any construction and/or sale of the illegally occupied property, and demolishing of any illegal construction already made by the neighbor.

f. File a complaint to the municipal corporation (such as MCD in Delhi) against illegal trespass of our property by the neighbors, with proofs such as photos. This is also applicable if some construction has been made by the neighbors without proper planning permission.

g. File a written complaint before the sub divisional magistrate (SDM) with proofs.

h. File a civil suit for damages from the neighbors for illegal occupation of our property.

i. File a complaint with the revenue or land authorities to prevent mutation of land records by the neighbors.

Note that the above steps include both civil and criminal trespass.

5.13 Steps to take in case of extended civil trespass to property

Civil trespass comes under law of torts. Tort means a civil wrong, i.e. where a person harms or violates the civil rights of another. In this case, the wronged person can file a court case on the other for compensation for damages and losses incurred by the wronged person.

In case of illegal occupation of property, actions such as building unauthorized construction on another's land or property, denying someone access to their own property, for example by installing locks or gates, would come under the definition of trespass and would fall under tort law. Hence, the owners of such property can claim recovery of damages from the occupier. The same holds where a neighbor builds fences, gates or other construction that encroaches one's property.

However, as mentioned earlier, if the illegal occupation is accompanied by threats or violence by the occupier, it would fall under the category of criminal trespass and a police complaint can be filed.

5.14 Adverse possession and civil trespass

One must be extra careful, in case of trespass, to take action promptly before it is too late. Under Indian law, if a trespasser has been in continuous control over a property for 12 years, without any legal action by the rightful owner to eject the trespasser from the property, it is termed as "adverse possession".

Extract from the Wikipedia article on adverse possession: *In general, a property owner has the right to recover possession of their property from unauthorized possessors through legal action such as ejectment. However, in the English common law tradition, courts have long ruled that when someone occupies a piece of property without permission and the property's owner does not exercise their right to recover their property for a significant period of time, not only is the original owner prevented from exercising their right to exclude, but an entirely new title to the property "springs up" in the adverse possessor. In effect, the adverse possessor becomes the property's new owner.*

The idea behind the adverse possession law is that if the rightful owner does not take any action to claim the property or take care of the property for the time period specified, the law assumes that they are not interested in the property and hence the trespasser can be awarded the rights.

However, it is to be noted that if the rightful owner starts court proceedings to eject the trespasser from the illegal occupied property before the 12 years of continuous occupation are over, then the time from the beginning of the illegal occupation would not be counted at all in the 12 years, as long as the legal proceedings are ongoing.

Therefore, if one's property is being trespassed by an illegal occupier, it is best to initiate the court proceedings as soon as possible.

It is best to ensure that illegal occupation does not take place right from the onset. For this, the rightful owner should keep checking on it regularly to make sure that illegal construction is not being made on the property. They should, if needed, construct boundary walls on the property to deter illegal possession. It is far easier in terms of effort, time and money to prevent illegal possession than to take legal actions to eject the possessor from the property later. Even after the court has given an order to eject the illegal trespasser from the property, its execution can sometimes also be a problem.

In India, adverse possession and illegal possession can be a major issue with NRIs who may be working for many years in a foreign country and not checking on their own land regularly. However, it may also happen due to unscrupulous relatives or others who may have designs on the property.

5.15 Encroachment and Municipal Response

Encroachment is a common form of trespass in Indian cities where individuals extend boundaries illegally onto public or private land. Municipal authorities have the power to demolish such encroachments under relevant local laws. However, evictions must follow due process, including adequate notice and rehabilitation if required.

Citizens affected by encroachment may file:

- Civil suits for possession and damages
- Complaints to the municipality for removal
- Public Interest Litigations (PILs) in case of large-scale land grabs

5.16 Adverse Possession

Adverse possession allows a person to claim legal ownership of land if they have occupied it openly, continuously, and hostilely for a specific statutory period (typically 12 years under the Limitation Act).

Requirements:

- Continuous possession without permission
- Open and notorious use
- Hostile to the true owner's interest

This doctrine has been criticized for enabling land grabbers but also supports cases where settlers have built lives over decades without legal title. Courts now approach such claims cautiously, especially when filed against public land.

5.17 Landmark Indian Cases on Trespass

- K.K. Verma v. Union of India (1954): Affirmed that any unauthorized entry, however slight, amounts to trespass.

- Krishna Ram Mahale v. Shobha Venkat Rao (1989): Recognized right to privacy in domestic space; expanded civil trespass to include unwanted intrusion.

- State of Rajasthan v. Mst. Vidhyawati (1962): Held the state liable for negligence and trespass by its employees.

These cases shaped the evolving contours of the right to possession, privacy, and state accountability.

5.18 Defence in Trespass Cases

Common defences include:

- **License**: Express or implied permission to enter.

- **Necessity**: Entry to prevent harm, e.g., to rescue someone in danger.
- **Statutory Authority**: Entry by government officers or utilities for official purposes.

However, such defences are interpreted strictly, especially when the right to property is infringed.

5.19 Prevention and Practical Advice

- Mark boundaries and put up clear signage
- Maintain records of property ownership
- Avoid informal tenancy arrangements
- Install security systems and CCTVs
- Keep copies of any permissions or notices

Proactive measures reduce litigation and strengthen one's legal position in court.

5.20 Conclusion

Trespass law is not just about physical entry—it encompasses modern challenges from drone surveillance to urban encroachments. As real estate disputes rise and privacy becomes a major concern, courts and citizens alike must remain vigilant in asserting and defending property rights.

Trespass guards possession. But some wrongs, like false accusations or maliciously using the courts, go beyond physical space. These are covered under malicious prosecution, the focus of the next chapter.

Chapter 6: Tort of Malicious Prosecution

In this chapter we discuss the tort of malicious prosecution.

6.1 What is Malicious Prosecution

The tort of malicious prosecution is the malicious institution of unsuccessful criminal or bankruptcy or liquidation proceedings against a person without a reasonable or probable cause.

The tort of malicious prosecution balances two competing principles:

- Freedom that every person should have in bringing criminals to justice
- The need for restraining false accusations against innocent persons.

Malicious prosecution is an abuse of the process and time of the court and an abuse of the judicial system by wrongfully setting the law in motion on a criminal charge against the person. If this is not prevented, innocent people would be convicted and the faith of the public in the judicial system would be shaken. That is why, this tort is taken seriously by the Indian courts.

The reasoning behind this tort of malicious prosecution lies in the abuse of the process of the court by wrongfully setting the law in motion and is designed to encourage the perversion of the machinery of justice for a proper cause.

The tort of malicious prosecution provides a redress for those who are prosecuted without cause and with malice.

6.2 Proof of Malicious Prosecution

In an action for malicious prosecution, the plaintiff must prove the following had happened:

- That they were prosecuted by the defendant.
- That the prosecution proceeding was terminated in favor of the present plaintiff.
- That the prosecution was instituted against them without any just or reasonable cause
- That the prosecution was instituted with a malicious intention i.e., not with the mere intention of bringing the law into effect but with an intention which was wrongful in fact. Malicious intention can be proved by things such as false evidence in the prosecution complaints.
- That the plaintiff suffered damage to their reputation or to the safety of their person or to the security of their property as a result of the malicious prosecution against them by the defendant.

6.3 Remedies for Malicious Prosecution

If the above are proved, then the court may award remedies for the tort including a sum of money as damages, injunction, restitution of property lost and other legal remedies.

6.4 IPC Section 211 in the Indian Penal Code for False Charge of Offence with Intent to Injure

Bringing false criminal charges against the plaintiff can also be a crime as per the Indian Penal Code IPC. Section 211 of the IPC states the following:

211. False charge of offence made with intent to injure.— Whoever, with intent to cause injury to any person, institutes or causes to be instituted any criminal proceeding against that person, or falsely charges any person with having committed an offence, knowing that there is no just or lawful ground for such proceeding or charge against that person, shall be punished with imprisonment of either description for a term which may extend to two years, or with fine, or with both; and if such criminal proceeding be instituted on a false charge of an offence punishable with death, imprisonment for life, or imprisonment for seven years or upwards, shall be punishable with imprisonment of either description for a term which may extend to seven years, and shall also be liable to fine.

Therefore, if a false criminal case is proved against the defendant, they may be liable for action by the police as per IPC Section 211. This is in addition to the civil remedies that are applicable as per the tort of malicious prosecution.

Malicious prosecution reminds us that the legal system itself can become a weapon. Understanding how tort law interacts with the civil procedure code helps us better defend our rights — as we'll now see.

Chapter 7: Code of Civil Procedure

In this chapter we discuss the code of civil procedure, which covers the laws in India related to torts.

THE CODE OF CIVIL PROCEDURE, 1908

ACT No. 5 OF 1908[1]

[*21st March*, 1908.]

An Act to consolidate and amend the laws relating to the procedure of the Courts of Civil Judicature.

WHEREAS it is expedient to consolidate and amend the laws relating to the procedure of the Courts of Civil Judicature : It is hereby enacted as follows : —

PRELIMINARY

1. Short title, commencement and extent.—(*1*)This Act may be cited as the Code of Civil Procedure,1908.

(*2*) It shall come into force on the first day of January, 1909.

---

1. This Act has been amended in its application to Assam by Assam Acts 2 of 1941 and 3 of 1953; to Tamil Nadu by Madras Act 34 of 1950, Madras A.O. 1950, and Tamil Nadu Act 15 of 1970; to Punjab by Punjab Act 7 of 1934; to Uttar Pradesh by U.P. Acts 4 of 1925, 35 of 1948, 24 of 1954, 17 of 1970, 57 of 1976 and 31 of 1978; to Karnataka by Mysore Act 14 of 1955; to Kerala by Kerala Act 13 of 1957; to Rajasthan by Rajasthan Act 19 of 1958; to Maharashtra by Maharashtra Act 22 of 1960 and 25 of 1970; It has been extended to Berár by the Berar Laws Act, 1941 (4 of 1941) and, by notification under ss. 5 and 5A of the Schedule Districts Act, 1874 (14 of 1874), also to the following Scheduled Districts :—

(*1*) The district of Jalpaiguri, Cachar (excluding the North Cachar Hills Goalpara (including the Eastern Duars),Kamrup, Darrang, Nowgong (excluding the Mikir Hill Tracts) Sibsagar (excluding the Mikir Hill Tracts) and Lakhimpur (excluding the Dibrugarh Frontier Tracts) : Gazette of India, 1909, Pt. 1. p. 5 and *ibid*, 1914, Pt

Figure 1. First page of the code of civil procedure 1908 (includes laws related to torts)

7.1 Introduction to the Code of Civil Procedure

The code of civil procedure was instituted in British India in 1908 as a consolidation of previous codes such as an earlier version from 1858. The same code has subsisted in independent India with a few amendments.

The code of civil procedure includes the following:

- General principles of jurisdiction of civil cases
- The rules and procedures for different kinds of lawsuits and the procedure for appeals.

These are applicable mainly for civil court cases in Indian courts.

7.2 Relevant extracts from the code of civil procedure

Extracts from the code of civil procedure that are relevant to tort law, are as follows:

16. Suits to be instituted where subject-matter situate.— Subject to the pecuniary or other limitations prescribed by any law, suits— (a) for the recovery of immovable property with or without rent or profits, (b) for the partition of immovable property,

Provided that a suit to obtain relief respecting, or compensation for wrong to, immovable property held by or on behalf of the defendant may, where the relief sought can be entirely obtained through his personal obedience, be instituted either in the Court within the local limits of whose jurisdiction the property is situate, or in the Court within the local limits of whose jurisdiction the defendant actually and voluntarily resides, or carries on business, or personally works for gain

19. Suits for compensation for wrongs to person or movables.—Where a suit is for compensation for wrong done to the person or to movable property, if the wrong was done within the local limits of the jurisdiction of one Court and the defendant resides, or carries on business, or personally works for gain, within the local limits of the jurisdiction of another Court, the suit may be instituted at the option of the plaintiff in either of the said Courts.

7.3 Conclusion

Procedure empowers substance. Once civil procedure is clear, we move toward practical action — like sending a legal notice. The next chapter explains how.

Chapter 8: Sending a Legal Notice

In case of repeated tort violations, such as by one's neighbors, it may be worth sending a legal notice to the violator to cease the action by a certain timeline, failing which further legal and other steps will be taken. If this issue is resolved early, unnecessary legal costs and hassle can be avoided.

8.1 How to send a legal Notice

It is better to get the legal notice drafted by an advocate in one's city on their letterhead and send it through a government run recorded post such as registered post or speed post. The legal notice should have details of the action committed with a specific date and time, and contain a request to cease the action, failing with further legal steps will be taken.

8.2 A sample legal notice

A sample legal notice has the following format:

<Advocate's letterhead with the legal firm's name and address>

Through Registered Post/ Speed Post

Legal Notice

Date<>

To <complete name and address>

Dear Sir/Madam,

Under instructions from our clients <name and address>, we are instructed to address you as under:

That We/my client are/is the resident of <address of housing or flat>

That On <date and time>, you performed the following actions <specific details of the actions such as encroachment of property>.

That We had raised the issue on <date> verbally and via a letter, but despite the warning you did not <details of actions>.

That You are hereby instructed, by way of this legal notice, to perform the following corrective actions <list of corrective actions such as removing encroachments> within this date <date>.

Failure to comply with this notice within the specified date will result in further legal actions to be taken against you as per the law. You will be liable for the costs of any such legal actions.

Yours faithfully:

<Signature and if possible, stamp of advocate>

Copy to: <Housing association>

8.3 Conclusion

Issuing a legal notice is often the first step in asserting a tort claim. But where harm occurs through others — like employees, agents or contractors — the law of vicarious liability governs. That is our next topic.

Chapter 9: Vicarious Liability

Vicarious liability is a foundational concept in tort law that holds one person liable for the wrongful acts of another. This liability typically arises in relationships where one person exercises control or authority over the other, such as employer-employee or principal-agent relationships. The rationale is that the controlling party is in the best position to prevent harm or compensate for it.

9.1 Meaning and Scope

The term vicarious liability comes from the Latin phrase *respondeat superior*, meaning "let the master answer." Under this principle, an employer is held liable for the torts committed by an employee if the act was done in the course of employment. This concept also applies to other relationships where one party can be said to act on behalf of another.

The scope of vicarious liability has broadened over time to include liability for negligent acts, intentional torts, and even some criminal acts, provided they were done during the course of employment or agency.

9.2 Conditions for Vicarious Liability

To establish vicarious liability, the following essential conditions must be met:

- **Existence of a qualifying relationship**: Typically employer-employee, but also principal-agent, partners, state-citizen, etc.
- **Wrongful act**: The act must constitute a tortious act (e.g., negligence, assault, defamation).
- **Act done in the course of employment**: The act must be sufficiently connected with the duties of the job.

For example, if a delivery driver negligently injures a pedestrian while making deliveries, the employer can be held liable.

9.3 Key Case Laws

- **State of Rajasthan v. Vidhyawati (AIR 1962 SC 933)**: A government driver's negligence resulted in a pedestrian's death. The court held the state vicariously liable, highlighting that the state, when engaged in non-sovereign functions, is liable like any other employer.
- **Limpus v. London General Omnibus Co. (1862)**: Even though the driver had specific instructions not to race other buses, his employer was still held

liable because he was acting within the general scope of his employment.

- **ICICI Bank v. Shanti Devi Sharma (2008)**: Recovery agents engaged by the bank misbehaved with a borrower. The court held the bank liable for the agents' misconduct, noting that liability arises even when unlawful methods are employed in the course of authorized work.

- **Chairman, Railway Board v. Chandrima Das (2000)**: A foreign national was raped by railway employees in a government building. The Supreme Court held the Union of India liable, treating the act as part of its non-sovereign functions.

9.4 Exceptions and Defences

While vicarious liability is a strict form of liability, there are exceptions:

- **Frolic of his own**: If an employee acts entirely outside the scope of employment for personal reasons, the employer may not be held liable.

- **Independent contractors**: Usually, a principal is not vicariously liable for the acts of independent contractors, unless the work is inherently dangerous or there is negligence in hiring.

- **Sovereign functions**: The state may be exempt from liability for certain core governmental functions (though this distinction is narrowing in India).

9.5 Extended Relationships

- **Principal and Agent**: A principal is liable for torts committed by an agent within the scope of the agent's authority.//
- **Partners in a Firm**: Under the Indian Partnership Act, each partner is liable for the acts of others done in the course of the business.
- **State Liability**: The state can be held liable for tortious acts by its employees when acting under non-sovereign capacities.

9.6 Practical Implications

Employers and principals must exercise due diligence in hiring, training, and supervising those who act on their behalf. Proper documentation, clear job descriptions, and compliance mechanisms can reduce exposure to vicarious liability.

9.7 Summary Table

Relationship	Liable Party	Conditions for Liability
Employer-Employee	Employer	Act in course of employment
Principal-Agent	Principal	Act within scope of agent's authority
Partners	Each partner	Act done in ordinary course of business
State-Citizen	State	Non-sovereign function, public duty breached

9.8 Conclusion

Vicarious liability plays an important role in ensuring accountability within hierarchical relationships. In India, courts have adopted an expansive view of this doctrine to better protect victims and uphold the principle of justice. As newer workplace and agency relationships emerge—gig workers, platform economies—the scope of vicarious liability is likely to expand further.

But beyond who is liable, we must ask — what remedies are available? The next chapter explores remedies and consumer compensation in tort law.

Chapter 10: Consumer Protection and Torts

The domain of consumer protection in India provides a complementary avenue for redressal of wrongs that would otherwise fall under tort law. With the enactment of the Consumer Protection Act, 2019, consumers are empowered to seek remedies for unfair trade practices, defective products, and deficient services—many of which align with tortious wrongs such as negligence and misrepresentation.

10.1 Relationship Between Tort Law and Consumer Protection

Tort law is judge-made law derived from common law principles, while consumer protection law is statutory. However, the overlap between them is substantial. Many harms that consumers suffer—such as bodily injury from a defective product or psychological harm from false advertising—can be addressed under both tort and consumer law. While tort law offers broader flexibility, consumer law offers faster redress through consumer commissions.

10.2 Key Features of the Consumer Protection Act, 2019

The 2019 Act expanded the scope of consumer rights in India. Salient features include:

- **Product Liability**: Manufacturers, sellers, and service providers can be held liable for harm caused by defective products or deficient services.
- **Consumer Rights**: Including the right to safety, information, choice, redressal, and consumer education.
- **E-commerce Regulation**: The Act extends protections to buyers of online goods and services.
- **Consumer Protection Councils and Redressal Forums**: Multi-tiered redressal systems including District, State, and National Commissions.
- **Central Consumer Protection Authority (CCPA)**: Empowered to take suo moto actions, investigate complaints, and recall unsafe goods.

10.3 Tortious Wrongs Covered Under Consumer Law

Many torts have parallels in consumer law:

- **Negligence**: A doctor's careless surgery or a builder's use of substandard materials.

- **Misrepresentation**: False claims in product advertisements or warranties.
- **Defamation and Unfair Trade Practices**: In certain commercial contexts.

10.4 Case Laws and Judicial Precedents

- **Indian Medical Association v. V.P. Shantha (1995)**: The Supreme Court ruled that medical services fall under the Consumer Protection Act, thus bringing medical negligence under its purview.
- **Spring Meadows Hospital v. Harjot Ahluwalia (1998)**: Both hospital and doctors were held liable for a negligent injection administered to a child.
- **Kavita Ahuja v. Shipra Estates (2016)**: The National Commission held a builder liable for delay in possession, setting important precedent for real estate disputes.

10.5 Practical Comparison: Tort vs Consumer Law

Aspect	Tort Law	Consumer Protection Law
Source	Common law (judicial precedents)	Statutory (Consumer Protection Act)

Forum	Civil courts	Consumer redressal commissions
Damages	Compensatory, punitive	Mostly compensatory
Cost and Time	Higher cost and longer duration	Lower cost and quicker resolution
Burden of Proof	Plaintiff must prove tort and damage	Complainant-friendly presumptions

10.6 Complementary Use of Tort and Consumer Law

Victims may choose either remedy, but in some cases, both forums can be approached, though not for duplicate relief. Tort law is preferable for:

- Seeking punitive damages
- Non-consumer harms (e.g., trespass, nuisance)
- Where the wrongdoer is not a "service provider"

Consumer law is more practical for routine grievances involving:

- Faulty goods or deficient services
- Medical negligence
- Real estate frauds

10.7 Tips for Consumers Seeking Remedies

- Preserve all documentation: invoices, warranties, prescriptions
- File complaints within the prescribed limitation period (2 years)
- Seek expert reports for establishing negligence
- Approach appropriate redressal forum based on claim value

10.8 Conclusion

Consumer protection law and tort law share common goals—compensating victims and deterring wrongful conduct. For Indian citizens, awareness of both legal tools is crucial for asserting their rights. As courts and commissions increasingly interpret the law in light of evolving commercial and technological contexts, the boundary between tort and consumer law will continue to shift, offering enhanced protection to individuals.

Remedies bring closure. Yet tort law, like any branch of law, continues to evolve with changing times and new harms. Our final chapter reflects on these evolving directions and possibilities in the digital age.

Chapter 11: Emerging Torts in the Digital Age

The rapid evolution of digital technology and online behaviour has given rise to new forms of harm that were not envisioned under traditional tort doctrines. As individuals increasingly interact, transact, and express themselves in the virtual space, courts and lawmakers are grappling with how to adapt tort principles to modern, digital-age wrongs.

11.1 Understanding Cyber Torts

Cyber torts refer to civil wrongs committed using digital technologies, particularly the internet. They often involve the violation of privacy, reputation, data security, or emotional well-being through online means. Common examples include:

- **Online Defamation**: Spreading false and damaging statements through social media, blogs, or news portals.

- **Cyberstalking and Harassment**: Repeated online contact that causes fear or distress.

- **Data Breach and Identity Theft**: Unauthorized access to personal or financial data.

- **Doxxing**: Public release of private or sensitive personal information without consent.
- **Impersonation or Deepfake Content**: AI-generated media used to mimic or damage someone's reputation.

11.2 Liability in the Digital Ecosystem

The digital world introduces new actors into the liability equation:

- **Individual Users**: Can be directly liable for defamatory or harassing content.
- **Platforms and Intermediaries**: Social media and tech companies may face limited liability under the IT Act, 2000, but recent changes require due diligence and grievance redress mechanisms.
- **Employers**: May be vicariously liable if an employee uses company resources or position to commit online torts.

11.3 Legal Framework and Challenges

While India does not have a codified cyber tort law, elements of redress can be found in:

- **Information Technology Act, 2000**: Addresses hacking, identity theft, and obscene content but is largely criminal in nature.
- **Indian Penal Code (IPC)**: Covers defamation (Sec 499–500), cyberstalking, and criminal intimidation.
- **Tort Law Principles**: Can be invoked for damages in civil suits, especially in cases of mental anguish, reputational loss, or privacy invasion.

Challenges:

- Difficulty in identifying anonymous perpetrators.
- Cross-border jurisdiction issues.
- Lack of awareness and under-reporting.
- Technical complexity in presenting digital evidence.

11.4 Case Law and Developments

- **Sabu Mathew George v. Union of India (2018)**: The Supreme Court directed internet intermediaries to block content violating laws against sex-selective abortion, illustrating judicial willingness to regulate online platforms.
- **Shreya Singhal v. Union of India (2015)**: Struck down Section 66A of the IT Act as unconstitutional

for violating free speech, but emphasized intermediary liability under due diligence.

- **SM Zaheer v. Union of India (2021)**: Delhi HC directed Facebook to take down defamatory posts, highlighting civil relief through tort law.

11.5 Global Trends and Indian Response

Countries like the US and EU are introducing specific frameworks like the Digital Services Act (EU) and stronger data protection laws. India's proposed **Digital India Act** and **Data Protection Act** may reshape the cyber tort landscape by:

- Creating a right to be forgotten
- Penalizing misuse of personal data
- Defining liability for AI-generated content

11.6 Practical Remedies and Tips

- Victims of cyber harm should collect digital evidence: screenshots, URLs, metadata.
- File police complaints (cybercrime portal) and civil suits for damages.
- Issue legal notices to perpetrators and intermediaries.

- Approach High Courts for writs in urgent reputation or privacy matters.

11.7 Need for Reform

India urgently needs a civil liability framework for digital harms:

- Codified cyber tort provisions
- Specialized cyber tribunals or courts
- Expanded definitions of reputation, privacy, and mental harm
- Balancing of free speech with digital responsibility

11.8 Conclusion

As technology redefines how harm is inflicted and experienced, tort law must evolve to offer meaningful remedies in the digital space. From online harassment to AI-based impersonation, emerging torts require robust legal frameworks, judicial innovation, and public awareness to ensure that the rights of digital citizens are protected in both letter and spirit.

Chapter 12: Conclusion

In this book, we have gone through the definition of tort, the different types of torts and the remedies for torts provided under Indian law.

The law of torts in India, though historically rooted in British common law, has steadily grown into a dynamic and evolving legal framework. With each chapter, we have seen how tort law has extended its reach — from personal injury and defamation to trespass, malicious prosecution, and even state accountability through constitutional torts.

As mentioned, a tort is a civil wrong for which the courts may grant remedies to the affected person to compensate them for their damages incurred. Many torts can have a criminal as well as a civil element to them, and both are handled in different ways as per the law.

In this book we have discussed important dimensions to torts:

- How torts intersect with **fundamental rights** and public law,
- How negligence doctrines adapt to **modern medical and infrastructural realities**,
- The role of **strict liability** in industries handling hazardous materials and emerging technologies,

- The growing need to assert claims through tools like **legal notices** and **procedural safeguards**,
- And the broader **philosophical shift** — from purely private wrongs to a system that also facilitates justice against powerful actors including the State.

As tort law continues to develop in India, challenges like digital defamation, AI-driven errors, environmental disasters, and custodial harms will demand fresh legal interpretations. The judiciary has shown willingness to evolve tort principles, especially in cases involving public interest and social justice.

Ultimately, tort law is not just about compensation — it is about restoring balance, deterring misconduct, and affirming human dignity. For students, legal professionals, and citizens alike, a deeper understanding of torts is not just an academic pursuit — it is a step toward building a fairer society.

It is hoped that this book will raise awareness of the relevant laws on tort in the general public and prove useful to people who are fighting tort related cases in Indian courts.

About the Author

Siva Prasad Bose is a writer of introductory guides on aspects of law in India and a retired electrical engineer with 30 years of experience in Uttar Pradesh Power Corporation Limited. He received his engineering degree from Jadavpur University, Kolkata and has a law degree from Meerut University, Meerut and a BSc from MMH College, Ghaziabad. His interests lie in the fields of family law, civil law, law of contracts, and areas of law related to power electricity related issues. He has written more than 20 books in Hindi and English on different aspects of laws.

Other Books by Siva Prasad Bose

Introduction to Wills and Probate

Senior Citizens Abuse in India

Introduction to Negotiable Instruments

Introduction to Marriage Laws in India

Neighbor Problems in India and what to do about them

Managing Court Cases with Mental Strength

Delays in Court Cases in India

Self-Publish Books and E-Books in India

Introduction to Patents and Patent Law in India

Introduction to Property Law in India

www.ingramcontent.com/pod-product-compliance
Lightning Source LLC
Chambersburg PA
CBHW070115230526
45472CB00004B/1275